Raffaele Cetto - Alessandro Franceschini **Time and Architecture**
Casa Galina by Giovanni Leo Salvotti

Index

Introduction by Cristian Uez
p. 7

Casa Galina: from architectural *divertissement* to popular icon by Raffaele Cetto
p. 9

Casa Galina, the last "classical" ruins by Alessandro Franceschini
p. 20

Questions about «Casa Galina»
p. 22

Architecture: ruins between time and eternity
p. 26

Leon Battista Alberti: time as "consuming" factor
p. 30

Georg Simmel: the fascination for ruins
p. 34

Marc Augé: The absence of contemporary ruins
p. 38

Lessons about Casa Galina
p. 42

Casa Galina. A photo essay
p. 53

Bibliographical references
p. 94

Credits
p. 96

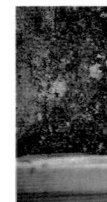

6

Introduction

Cristian Uez
Mayor of Calceranica al Lago (Trento)

For more than half a century, Calceranica's landscape has been characterised by the presence of a small yet significant building with unusual shapes, impossible to ignore: we are talking about the architecture brought to life by Giovanni Salvotti de Bindis and because of its original form, it was informally renamed Casa Galina from the beginning by my fellow citizens. When first built, this small architecture was surrounded by a very different landscape compared to today: the anthropization of Caldonazzo's lake shores was yet to come and the building's shapes reflected in those sweet fresh waters, in a mainly agricultural and rural context.

Highly recognizable, Casa Galina had an immediate sensational effect on the residents' collective imagination: with unprecedented shapes, this construction was destined to distinguish its surroundings for its capacity to stimulate the deep fantasies of those who passed by. Still today, even though the Casa Galina is hidden by other buildings and surrounded by dense vegetation, likewise to an ancient ruin, its symbolic role did not cease to exist, making it one of the characteristic elements of this territory in its own right. Casa Galina therefore deserves some reflection as regards to its restructuring and its original configuration. In the scope of a project that could give a new meaning to this architecture. This book intends to represent a first step in this direction.

Together with two critical papers which give an insight of the architectural and cultural context of the 20th century, this work collects vintage images, virtual reconstructions of the building and a photographic report describing its current state of abandonment. By looking through the book we are not only fascinated by a sense of nostalgia as well as a desire to understand and re-evaluate Casa Galina also arises. It is to be hoped that in the near future the building finds a new dimension, a new life, that allows it to increase the already numerous attractions of our beautiful territory.

8

Casa Galina: from architectural *divertissement* to popular icon

Raffaele Cetto

1. The project's origins

*It is impossible
for the same thing
to belong and not to belong
at the same time
to the same thing
and in the same respect.*
(1005 b 19-20) Aristotle

Summer of 1962 was not particularly warm in the city of Trento: also due to the heavy rain, the average temperature in July and August was 21,8 °C. It was probably in that period, to fight the boredom of a rainy Sunday, that Gian Leo Salvotti sketched for the first time an idea of what would become the Casa Galina for everybody in the town of Calceranica.

At that time, the architect from Trento, moved by a recent trip to Notre-Dame du Haut by Le Corbusier, was convinced about the possibility of creating works of architecture totally free in their form, unleashed from the building's tectonics. However, this is not enough to understand the origin and structure of the small dwelling house: during the 60's, secularisation became central again in social studies and in the field of architecture; we assisted to the desacralisation of works of art, to the loss – in their creative act – of all references to the Truth and the Absolute. For an architect who is also a philosopher, whose creed is based on Aristotle's principle of non- contradiction, this attitude is not only wrong but has to be opposed. Through Casa Galina, Salvotti does not offer a truth, rather he sacralizes a game: he takes away from the relative to give to the absolute, he replaces maieutics with irony, trying to make his contemporaries – and us – understand that beyond mere shape there is much more. If we acknowledge the epistemological value of this small building placed on the lake banks of Caldonazzo, we are able to better understand not only the work itself but also its construction system.

The experiences of the XXth century: Ronchamp

*...Ronchamp's church is baroque,
not for its resort to seventeenth-century shapes
but for the meaning that
D'Ors gave to Baroque when
he exultantly defined it as*

> «the persistent barbaric style, permanent in culture»
> G.C. Argan, 1956

Building started in September 1953 and was completed at the end of June 1955.
Notre-Dame du Haut's chapel generated a heated debate among the ecclesiastical and architectural circles in France, with a wrath of negative opinions: the new building in fact was defined as a "ecclesiastical garage", "slipper", "bunker" or "atomic bomb shelter" by several newspapers. This debate crossed the Alps and in October 1955 Ernesto Nathan Rogers dedicated the editorial of Casabella n°207 to Le Corbusier's method and his Chapelle de Ronchamp. The Director defines the chapel a masterpiece and praises its sculptural form, derived from the adherence to the context and the poetic interpretation of the functional needs expressed by the Sacred Art Commission of the Besançon's diocese. Roger's acclaim – echoed by Giuseppe Samonà and Bruno Zevi – was countered by Giulio Carlo Argan, who asked himself what could the meaning be, throughout Le Corbusier's coherent work, of "this construction so different from the others". For the Turinese critic it is all about a critical act, provocative in "its combination of shapes, opposite in their historical origins and semantic value" in which we can grasp "a taste for contamination and profanation… that offend me", stating that after the machine à habiter, the Swiss architect had patented a machine à prier. In the midst of this debate, Salvotti travelled to Notre-Dame de Haut, intrigued by the sculpture's expressivity through which Le Corbusier had apparently abandoned his rationalist principles, anticipating the Capitol Complex's scenographic symbolic inventions in Chandigarh. After reaching Ronchamp's hill, Salvotti found himself in front of an impressive building lacking any privileged point of observation and totally embedded in the landscape through its sinuous forms. Le Corbusier's choice for a totally expressive freedom is apparently contradictory to the principle of structural clarity: structural elements such as pillars, partitions in reinforced concrete and iron beams, are wrapped in membranes made by splashing mortar on wire meshes which serve both as disposable formworks and as a reinforcement. The roof as well

is made up of two thin layers (6 cm) of concrete which cover the seven flat beams inspired by the structures supporting the wings of an aircraft. This solution allows the Swiss architect to get free from the building's tectonics and to have total sculptural freedom in a way that emphasizes the poetic resonance of the landscape and shapes the requested liturgical programme.

The experiences of the XXth century: Baratti's Gulf

Nature works through spatial dimensions and tools instrumental to infinite solutions.
By learning the lesson and finding techniques kindred to nature in the realization of new projects means creating unexpected structures and rediscovering man's interior world: the inner dimensions are located in the human's organic structure, are fed by its biological functioning and therefore contained into a higher level of geometrical order. Therefore, man's psychic space finds its balance only in a space of equal measure.
Vittorio Giorgini

Le Corbusier once said that the idea for Ronchamp's covering came from the observation of one of his objets à réaction poétique: a crab's carapace found on a beach in Long Island during his stay in New York in 1946. Nature actively participates in the creation of la Chapelle by not only inspiring the Swiss architect in the volumes defining it but also by suggesting a few static solutions. In the same period, Florentine architect Vittorio Giorgini developed and theorized Spatiology: a discipline that aims to define a new architectural language based on technological innovation through the analysis of the relations between traditional planning and the work of nature. The 1st Manifesto of Spatiology was displayed at the 1st Triennale Itinerante d'Architettura Italiana Contemporanea held in Florence in 1965 to which Giorgini was invited thanks to the clamour resulting from the completion of his project for Casa Saldarini on the Baratti Gulf, near Piombino in Tuscany. Giorgini was fully aware of the Ronchamp project not only for its sculptural development but also for the structural solutions adopted. In his project, however, Giorgini takes Le Corbusier's membranes to a higher level: they do not wrap around the supporting structure, they are the supporting structure, becoming a single "isoelastic beam" giving shape to the entire building. In their construction process, the two buildings are similar, at least in relation to the membranes. Giorgini uses electro-welded wire meshes as well, overlapping several layers depending on the warp and stress, the whole thing stiffened by four centimetres of concrete. The building hovers in the air thanks to the thrust of three supports. In the project's design, the interior had to be an unicum, a real whale belly adherent and coherent with the supporting structure. The space was however divided into two sections – day and night - at the clients' request. It is curious how Giorgini never found an engineer who was willing to venture into the structure's calculations and had to finally go directly to empirical proof by building the structure.

Moreover, the test engineer, doubting the building's static, had the whole structure loaded with double the weight: the building not only held the weight but proved to be perfectly flexible. Like Ronchamp, Casa Saldarini was very controversial and it is fascinating that Giorgini, as well as Le Corbusier, were accused of creating a baroque building.

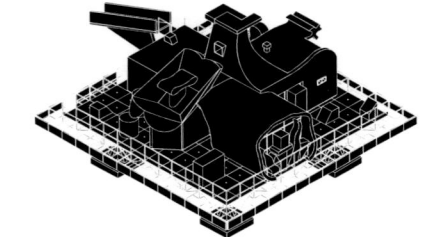

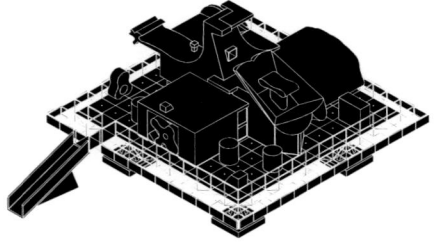

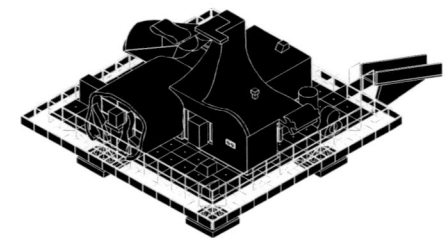

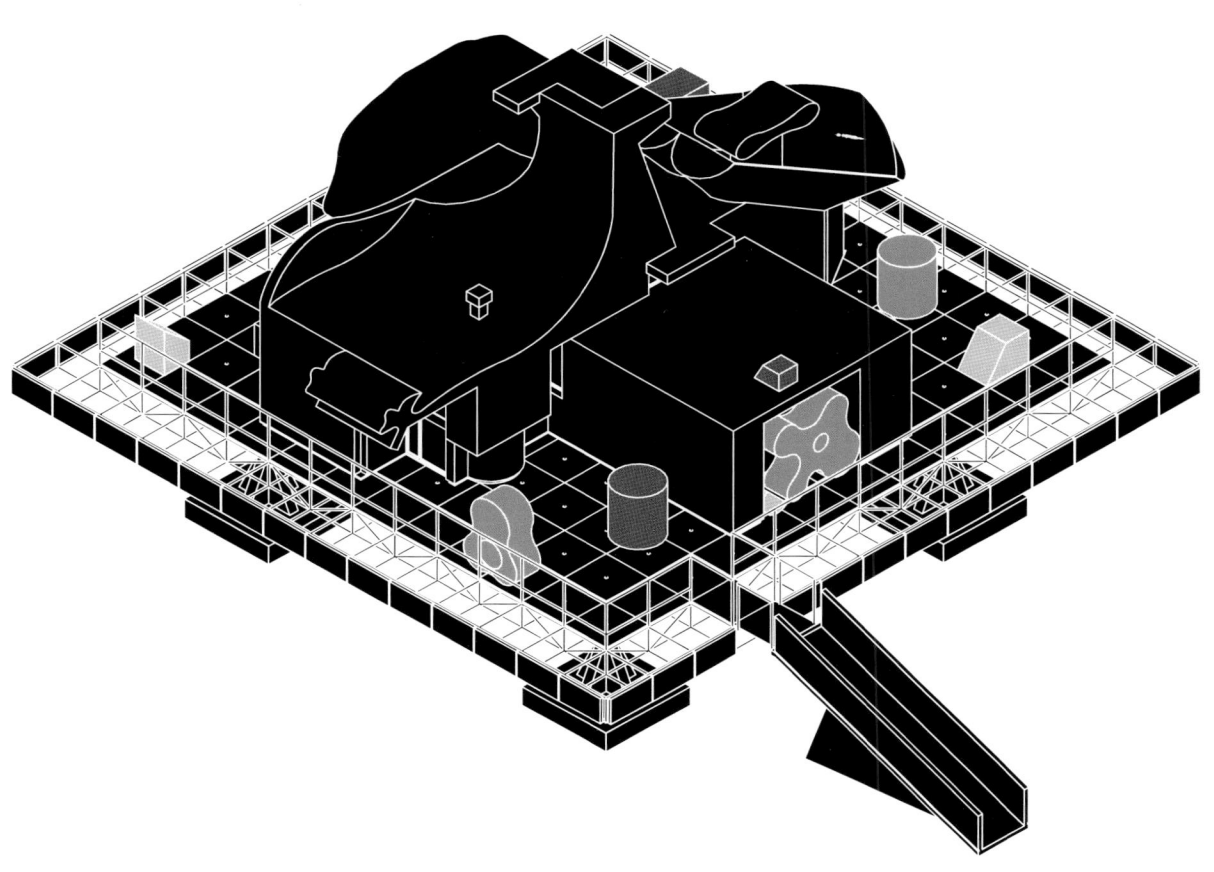

2. Casa Galina

The green light from the City Council of Calceranica al Lago for the construction of the small dwelling house by Giovanni Leo Salvotti was given on 8th February 1963. Therefore, the project is contemporary to the one of Casa Saldarini. Like Giorgini, Salvotti raises the ground level respect to the soil without however using a single structural system (the isoelastic beam) but overlapping three clearly distinct structural elements. The "membrane" system is used by Salvotti to freely design the volumes leaning on the metal platter which will give shape to Casa Galina.

Reinforced concrete
When works began in 1963, the landscape surrounding the land plots 659 and 660 of Calceranica's Council Land Registry was very different from today's: the lake shores were yet to be pushed back by the 60's and 70's building speculation and its waters almost reached the land chosen by Salvotti for his "game". The soil, although partially reclaimed, presented a few issues linked to humidity and the possibility that water would resurface in the case of heavy rain. It was also for this reason that the ground floor was risen, choosing to support it with four pillars in reinforced concrete, each one placed on a two square meter basis.
These pillars' design is very peculiar: the section is a Greek cross starting with arms 20 cm wide and 50 cm long. This latter extent is then reduced to 0 at a height of 105 cm from the foundation; at this point the cross makes a 45o rotation in order to extend its arms length until reaching 155 cm at the end. Finally, 20 cm before the end of the arms, four metallic "mushrooms" are anchored to the cross and on these lay the metallic structure above. Today, the structure is hidden behind the rampant parthenocissus and the hops. However, if we think of it free from vegetation, we can easily imagine these pillars almost dissolving, making the overhead structure rise. Another structure in reinforced concrete is the access ramp to the building: self-supporting, slightly longer than 5 meters and 120 cm wide, it is not anchored to the ceiling but connected to a one-metre long

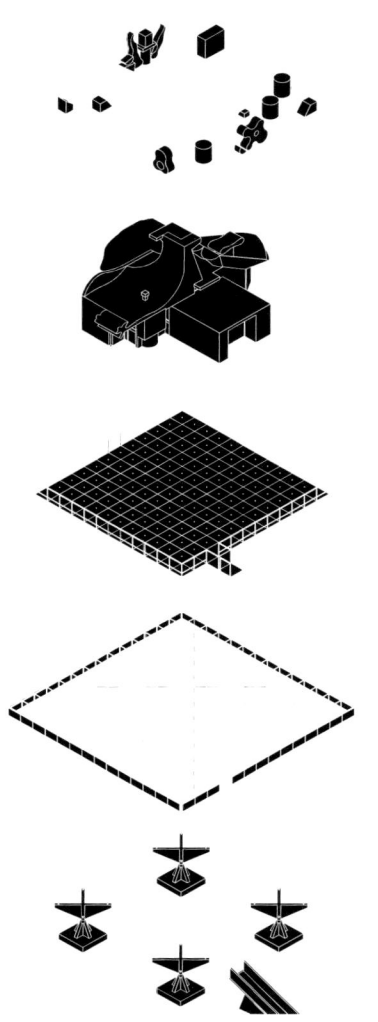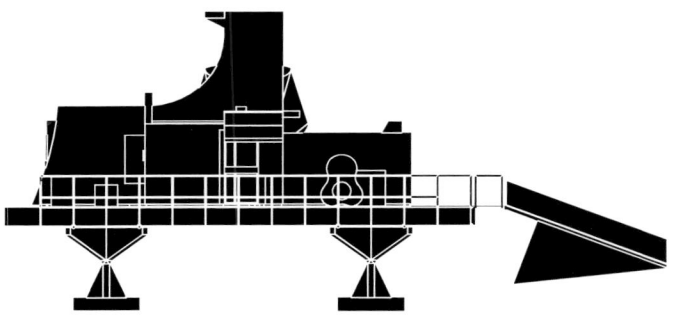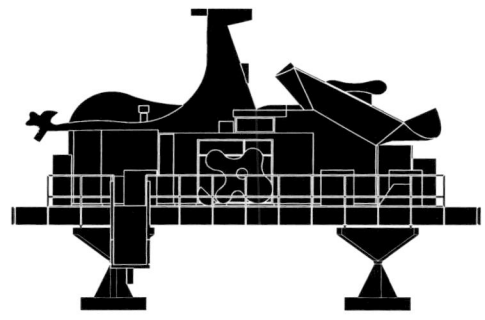

metal plate, as if the architect did not want to contaminate the sacredness of the "game".

Iron
The structure forming the game's platter is made in iron: by using 1.500 meters of black round tubular with a 35mm diameter, Salvotti created an orthogonal grid of 30 intertwined beams measuring 14 meters on each side. This grid was eventually fixed to the pillars with the four metallic "mushrooms", while its external borders were coated by 56 concrete plates five centimetres wide, each measuring 100x50 cm and painted white. The parapet, made with a white tubular with a diameter of 25mm, was then welded to this structure. It delimits a square of 12 meters per side paved with concrete plates which are always 5 cm wide, measuring 100x100 cm and with a 5cm hole in the middle that allows water to drain. With the alternation of black and white, these plates seem to recall the classic chessboard pattern.

Meshes
Once the board is completed, the pawns are still missing: as we can see from the original sketches, Salvotti had imagined a series of objects apparently placed in a random manner on the board from the beginning. These objects are meant to encircle the main volumes, on top of which stands the zoomorphic shape inspired by a horse, eventually transformed into a hen by the local residents' collective imagination. The designed figures are complex, difficult to reproduce with traditional techniques. To shape these figures, the architect chose to use electro-welded wire meshes with 10 cm pitches and an 8 mm diameter. By curving, bending, cutting and stitching these meshes, the iron workers made it possible to shape these figures in a laboratory and then carried them to the construction site once finished. Here, they were covered with a denser plaster mesh (2 cm pitches) on which a 5 cm wide structural concrete plaster would finally be placed. In this way, the figures become hollow self-supporting volumes. Salvotti decided to cover all the Casa Galina with tar: sometimes left exposed, painted in white in other spots, such as the main volume of the horse. As we can see from pictures of that time, some objects on the chessboard (flowers, cylinders, prisms) were painted with primary colours, suggesting that these pawns

are part of a game. In this way, Salvotti's desire to build a structure whose main task was to reaffirm – in architecture as well – the need to always relate to the truth and the absolute, was fulfilled.

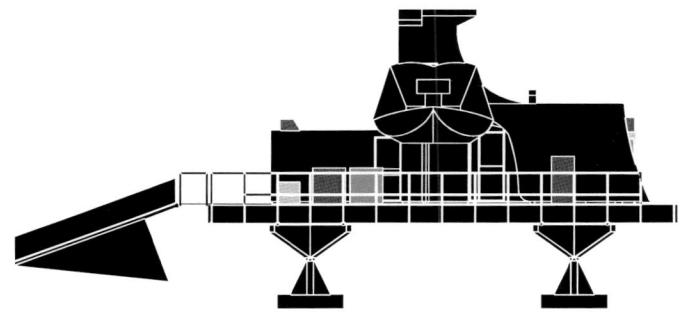

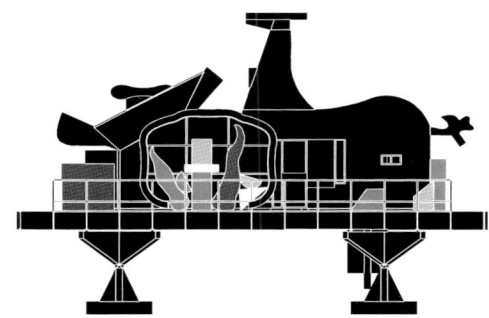

3. An icon in the collective imagination

When the project for Notre Dame du Haut was presented – in the form of a plaster model – it turned out to be difficult for the population, as well as for the Sacred Art Commission of the Besançon's diocese, which commissioned the work, to understand this type of architecture: misunderstandings, shock and concern emerged from the look at this unusual object, which did not refer to, in any way, the typically religious history. It is easy to imagine how the same astonishment had also hit those people who found themselves in front of Casa Saldarini or Casa Galina for the first time. Although this was not in the architect's plans, for the people from Piombino the small building designed by Giorgini almost immediately became Casa Balena ("the whale house") for its curvy lines recalling the shapes of a cetacean. Salvotti, instead, clearly wanted to evoke the shape of an animal: the sculptural volumes of his building represent a horse in the act of bending over a trough. However, for the local people, used to layered roofs and regular walls, that oddity, rather than horse-like seemed to represent a totally different animal. In a short time, in fact, not only in Calceranica but in all the region of Trentino, that building became Casa Galina: a strange construction run ashore a few meters from the water edge to be photographed and included in the album of a trip to the lake. The three buildings – Ronchamp, Casa Saldarini and Casa Galina – besides being similar for the sinuous shapes and the use of a similar techniques, appear to contain the same message: a heartfelt call for not getting accustomed to the daily greyness of bureaucracy, an incentive for the reawakening of being an architect and to find new approaches to solutions on a daily basis.

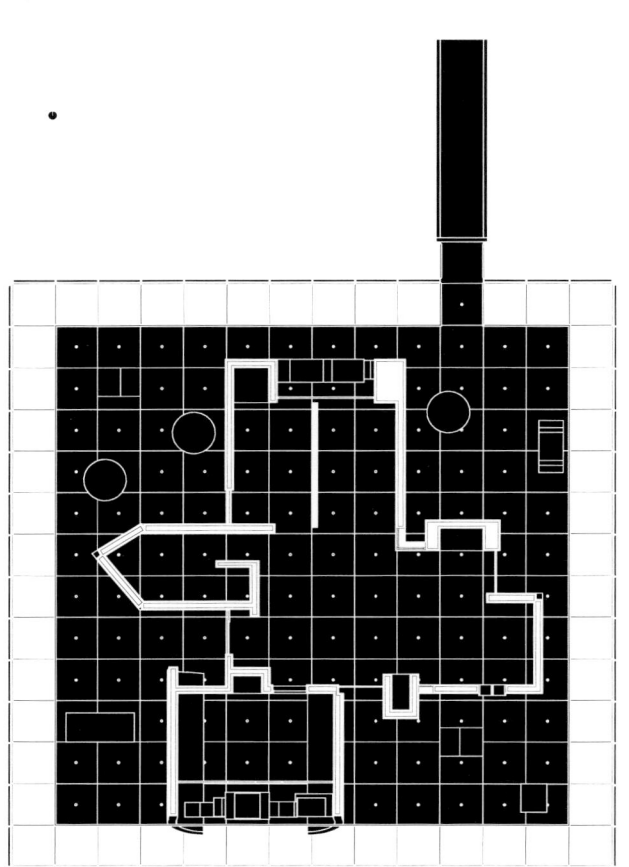
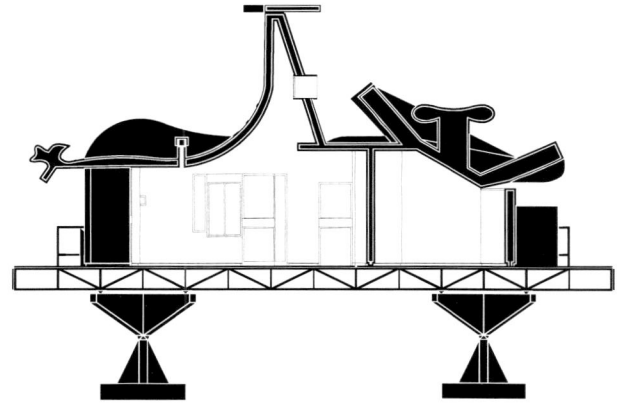

Casa Galina,
the last classical ruins

Alessandro Franceschini

Questions about «Casa Galina»

The existence of ruins like the ones at Casa Galina – a peculiar architectural ruin, since it was built only after the Second World War – opens the way to a few observations on the strengths of contemporary architecture with its relationship to time. Not only for the importance of this building in the local residents' collective imagination, but also because "ruins keep giving signs of life," in the words of Marc Augé (Augé, 2004, pag. 135). Although it has never been inhabited and even though it has been abandoned for decades, Casa Galina never actually gave up "living." Plants grow around Casa Galina luxuriously, making it appear like the living ruins of an ancient civilisation. However, they are unable to hide the many questions in this silent presence.

This small structure by the lake of Caldonazzo was built at the beginning of the 60's. By the author's own admission, the architect from Trentino Giovanni Leo Salvotti De Bindis, Casa Galina is an "architectural game". It is a zoomorphic-shaped structure with no specific function – besides the pretext of being a temporary holiday house – which faces history by means of its symbols. The author intended to evoke a horse while drinking. In the local residents' collective imagination instead, it assumes the bizarre shape of a chicken. But this is not the point: horse or chicken, these lines are in fact the composing pretexts to transform the traditional architectural shapes and to introduce new, unprecedented and bizarre developments.

This short essay wishes to include the experience of Casa Galina among the vast and very interesting literature on the subject of ruins as an excuse for developing philosophical thoughts over the transition of man on Earth, and the ephemerality of its actions. Without having the ambition of comprehensiveness, this essay tries to answer the questions that Casa Galina poses each time we look at it. Now that its shape has become formless and nature has quickly covered its beauty, Casa Galina firmly questions us on the founding issues of architecture under a new dimension, marked by the presence of modernity, but prematurely reduced to ruins.

Architecture: ruins between time and eternity

First of all, contemplating ruins means living the experience of time. A meaningful feeling only for the ones who are provided with the ability of "listening," without which the ruins can only appear silent, like a collection of disorganized wrecks. This listening ability is oriented towards the meaning of our transition on Earth and the meaning of time, and the ambition of human actions to last forever. The emotion provoked by these matters is given by the sense of caducity that they inspire and by comparing the mortality of men and things, where all ends up only a memory. As written by Lévi-Strauss in an inspired guess on the relationship between memory and undoing, "...by dragging my memories in its flow, Time has built, rather than consume or bury, with its fragments the solid foundations that provide my moving forward a more stable balance and clearer outlines to my sight" (Lévi-Strauss, 1982, pag. 42).

In this way, the ruins can be seen as an unfinished work of art gone back to nature, from which we can still draw lessons and emotions; actually, it provokes a strong sense of seduction in the human soul, because: "All men have a secret attraction to the ruins". These were the words of François-René de Chateaubriand at the beginning of the 19th century, trying to systematise an indescribable feeling: this attraction for decomposing architecture. "This feeling," he follows, "is due to the fragility of our nature, to a secret conformity between these destroyed monuments and the speed of our existence. In addition, there is an idea which comforts our littleness, seeing that whole nations, men sometimes so famous, have not yet been able to live beyond the few days assigned to our obscurity. So the ruins throw a great morality amid the scenes of nature" (de Chateaubriand, 1802). For the French philosopher Denis Diderot, instead, the ruins evoke subjective feelings like the universality of death, but allow at the same time to enable one to find himself again on top of the abyss, while all people and nations fall in it: "The ideas that ruins awake in me are great. Everything is annihilated, everything perishes, everything passes. Only the world remains. There is only time that lasts (...) A torrent leads nations one upon another, in the depths of a common abyss; me, I alone, I pretend to stop on the edge, and split the tide that flows by my side!" (Diderot, 1767, pag. 199). If this tide appears to position itself in an antithetic position compared to the human's actions' aim to the infinite, it is time itself to remind us: "Eternity is not a word that fits with human things" (Segre, 2003, pp. 120-121).

Leon Battista Alberti: time as "consuming" factor

Contemplating ruins in this way becomes a way to experience "time in its essence," with no date and no diachronic element. It also means to acknowledge the concept of history. To fully understand the role of architecture in the limited time of human events, it can be interesting to relate to Leon Battista Alberti's thoughts. Thanks to his studies on the Ancient Times, Alberti conceives an extraordinary vision of time and its relationship with the world lived in by humans. In "The Family in Renaissance Florence" (Libri della Famiglia) in particular, Alberti explains how time is an "invaluable thing," the real property of men "more than hands and eyes." A gift received together with the "...soul and body, from the first day," men spent on the Earth and destined to follow them until the last day. Alberti considers Time as made by two only apparently antithetic parts but in fact different features of the same view of the world. "Donor" and at the same time "Consumer" are the main characteristics of the Time dimension in which man is immersed. First of all, Time is donor. Thanks to it, Man can take action in the world, can dedicate himself to the study of bonae artes, to exercise the virtus, to family planning and to city-building. "Man, for Alberti, is ontologically temporary: only in time – an amount of time absolutely limited by birth and death – can its actions be practiced" (Cassani, 2000, pag. 22). Among these, we can find one of the most important actions, that is making architecture and leave it to the passing of Time.

Time is also inseparably consumer of all things, as we learn from Alberti. Following the model known since the ancient time and used through the Middle Ages and then during the Humanism period, Time is *tempus edax*. Time "takes away the goods from men with its flowing, it consumes Man's endeavours and cancels through oblivion the same litterarum monumenta, illusorily and unwisely considered eternal". "How could you believe that a brickwork would be eternal? ", affirms one of Alberti's main characters: "You should have known that even the greatest monuments of our cultural tradition are subject to ruin and destruction! "(Alberti, pag. 101). A consuming Time, able, therefore, to destroy monumental architectures very quickly.

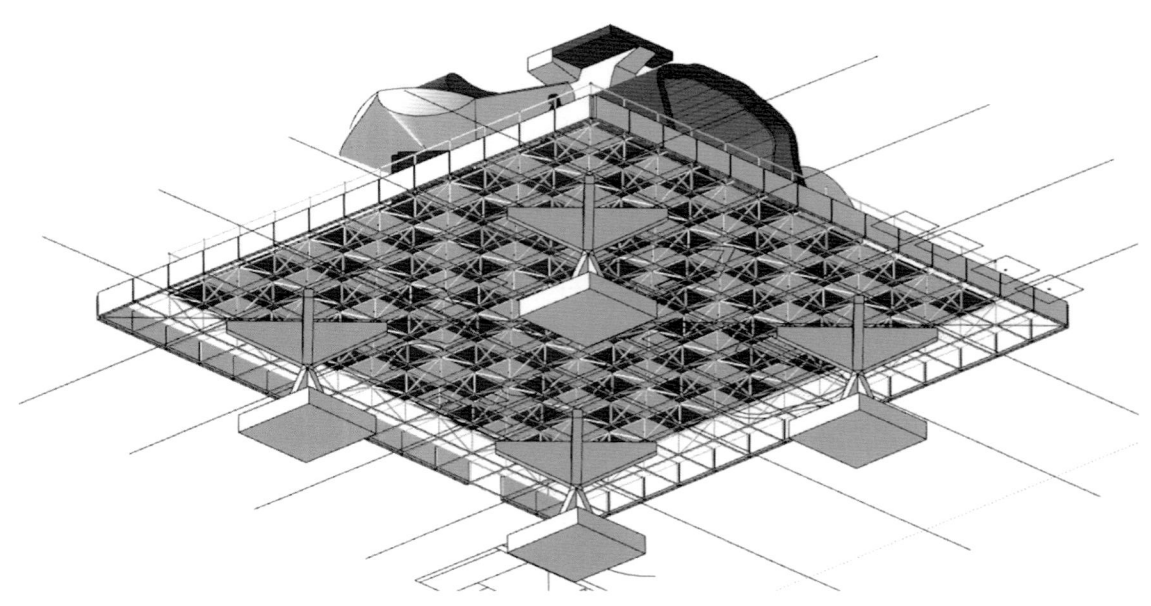

**Georg Simmel:
the fascination for ruins**

The aesthetic interpretation of ruins received a decisive impulse with Georg Simmel. According to the German philosopher, "the charm of ruins in last analysis lies in the fact that a work of art made by man can be perceived as a product of nature" (1919) and of its destructive power. Simmel's theory is that in the case of ruins, the timeless dimension of a work of art reunites with the temporal dimension of nature. An encounter of great symbolic power first intercepted by Giovanni Battista Piranesi and then part of a speculative concept in Simmel's work. The melancholy resulting from the view of ruins "is especially given by the fragility of nature, which has been readmitted in the space once precluded. The intact construction had violently cut out nature in pieces then filled up by the work of men" (Pacioni, 2015, pag. 29).

Simmel sees in ruins the presence of what Nicola Cusano called *coincidentia oppositorum,* between construction and destruction, between the work of man and nature's needs, which he identifies in the struggle between the spirit's will and the force of gravity, intended as the main effect of nature's brute and corrosive power. In Simmel's view, ruins cannot only be intended as the consequence of human demolition, or simply the decay of those physical matters with which architectures are built. In this scope, ruins gain their cultural significance only if able to live that natural process denying the spirit's architectural creations.
In this way, nature becomes the necessary instrument to transform the work of man into a ruin. Decadence is therefore seen as a dialectic process where ruins are the result of the integration between human projects and the process of nature, within an inevitable destiny. To say it in the words of Camus, "by losing the gloss imposed by man, ruins have returned to nature" (Camus, 1988, pag. 60).
In this vision, Simmel introduces a new concept of time, able to go backwards on itself: "as present shapes the past, ruins are able to collapse temporality. We are asked to contemplate the past in the present in the same way as the ruins represented the present in the past" (Simmel, 1919, pag. 135). Ruins therefore get involved in a process of meanings in which the latter are led to destruction. The return to nature of these structures created by man can aesthetically be seen in this vision as a backwards movement in time and the return of man's work to its original dimension. After losing its sense of being architecture, it finally endures a progressive decline until nature's action makes it go back to be a work of art in the form of ruins. Without nature's overwriting, these ruins are destined to lose themselves and turn into dust.

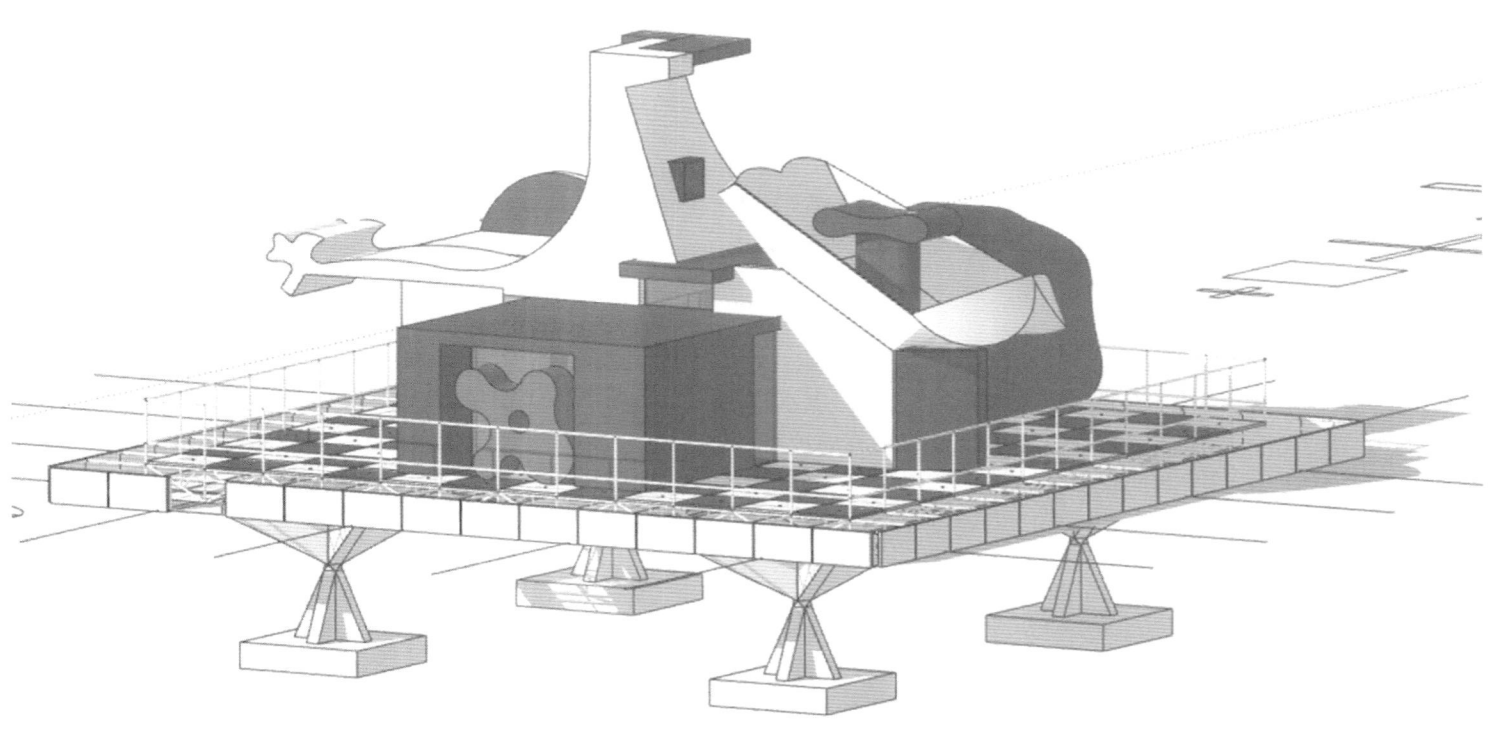

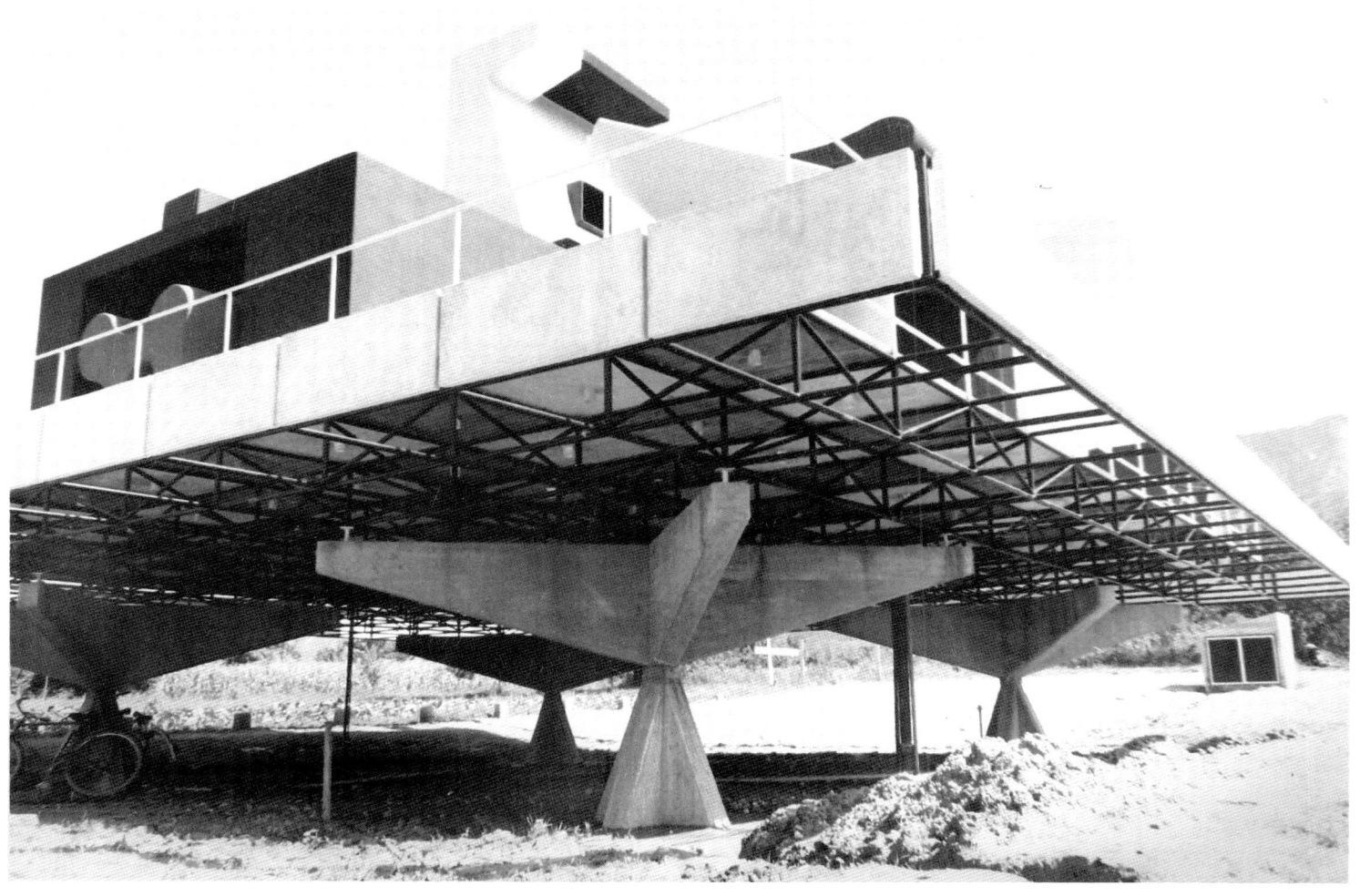

Marc Augé: the absence of contemporary ruins

In recent times, Marc Augé is among those who have made important reflections on the subject: "Ruins are the culmination of Art, in the way that multiple pasts to which they refer to incompletely double their enigma, while exacerbating their beauty. The originality of this world as a planet depends on this enigma's movement, that some contemporary artists have grasped" (Augé, 2004, pag. 138), and again, "The view of ruins makes us fleetingly realize the existence of a time which is not the one described in the history manuals or that restorations try to revive. It is a time (…) that is absent from our world made of images, simulacrums and reconstructions, from this violent world whose rubbles don't even have the time to become ruins. A lost time that Art is sometimes able to rediscover" (Augé, 2004, pag. 8).

For the French ethnologist as well, one of the fundamental elements for architecture to become a ruin is the slow action of time, real moulder (not a word in English) able to give new meanings to rubble. Augé writes: "In relation to the past, history is too vast, varied and profound to reduce itself to the mark on rock that has arisen, another lost object like the ones found by archaeologists, diggers of space-time slices. In regards to the present, the emotion is of an aesthetic kind but the show of nature combines with the one of the vestiges. We happen to contemplate landscapes from which we receive an intensely vague feeling of happiness; the more those landscapes are natural (the less they owe to the work of man), the more we are aware of its sense of permanence, compared to the ephemeral fate of all individuals" (Augé, 2004, pag. 37).

Contemplating ruins is therefore not the same as a journey through history but is "making the experience of time, of its pure essence." In this way, nature's endless renewal can be linked to the comforting feeling of "a totality transcending those fates, or in which the latter merge, the pantheist or materialistic intuition that 'nothing is created, nothing is destroyed.' In this sense, Nature not only removes history: it removes time" (Augé, 2004, pag. 37). This force, able to create an utterly, all-embracing bond between time and architecture, is the true protagonist in the transformation into ruins of the Vitruvio's art, with the consequent new symbolic meaning it interprets again. However, Augé warns us that modernity is characterized by the absence of time: this is why contemporary mankind is "unable to make ruins".

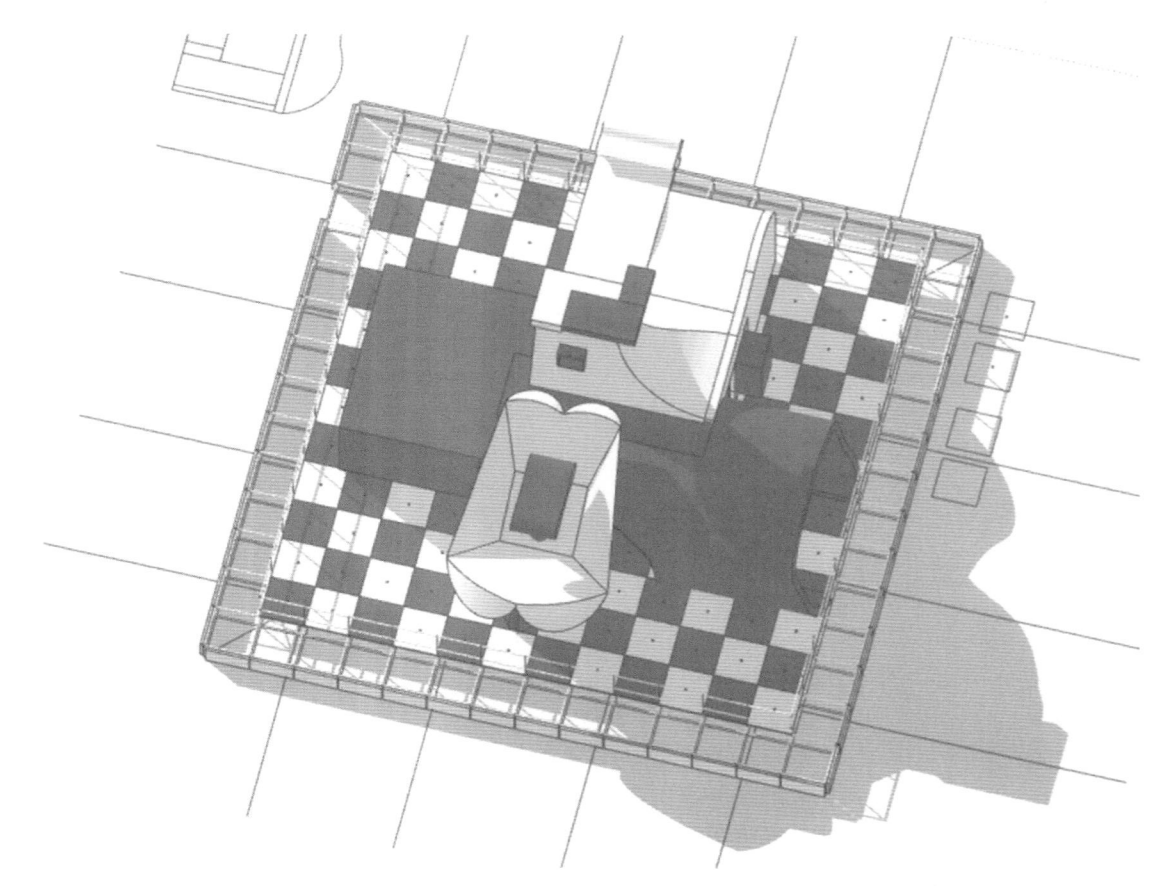

Lessons about Casa Galina

Marc Augé's warning is not valid for Casa Galina by architect Giovanni Salvotti. Here, in fact, all the elements necessary for the existence of the ruin itself are present. The architecture is now reduced to rubble and nature has exuberantly taken possession of it; there is also a symbolic overwriting inscribed in the local residents' collective imagination. If ruins are, in Franco Purini's words, "the convergence point of all the reflections on the ephemerality of human ambitions, on the ultimate fate of all architecture challenging Time, architecture that will inevitably break up against its own limits" (Purini, 2010, pag. 153), the Casa Galina is eligible to be the perfect interpreter of an aesthetic and philosophical dimension with a great symbolic power. Because "time is to eternity as the becoming of the sensitive world is to an intelligible being" (Snodgrass, 2004, pag. 71).

If "ruins are," in Purini's words, "the conceptual space in which beauty, if present, shows itself, in its naked truth" (Purini, 2010, pag. 153), then we can find at least three levels of interpretation suggested by the little relict of Casa Galina: the first argues that architecture is unable to last through time, has a low level of resilience and therefore suffers more the passing of days; the second suggests that contemporary architecture could not outlive its author, creating an unprecedented circumstance in the history of mankind, which has always seen in architecture a way to eternalise the architect's gesture; the third lesson finally affirms that contemporary architecture, when transformed into ruins, has nothing to envy, under an aesthetic perspective, to the ruins of ancient times, only as long as they fulfil the necessary conditions we discussed about. Lastly, we can also find a political message in Casa Galina's resistance to the passing of time and in its being a fully-fledged ruin of the modern world. "We can talk about authenticity of ruins in a modern way only if we look at them for what they are aesthetically and politically as architectures but also for the spatial and temporal doubts that modernity has always had for itself (…), an imaginary of ruins shall prove fundamental for every theory on modernity which aims to something higher than a mere exaltation of the achievements in the technological and scientific fields" (Huyssen, 2010). That is why Casa Galina, with its discrete presence, maybe represents a fundamental element to try to write about, in the future one day, the history of modern ruins.

46

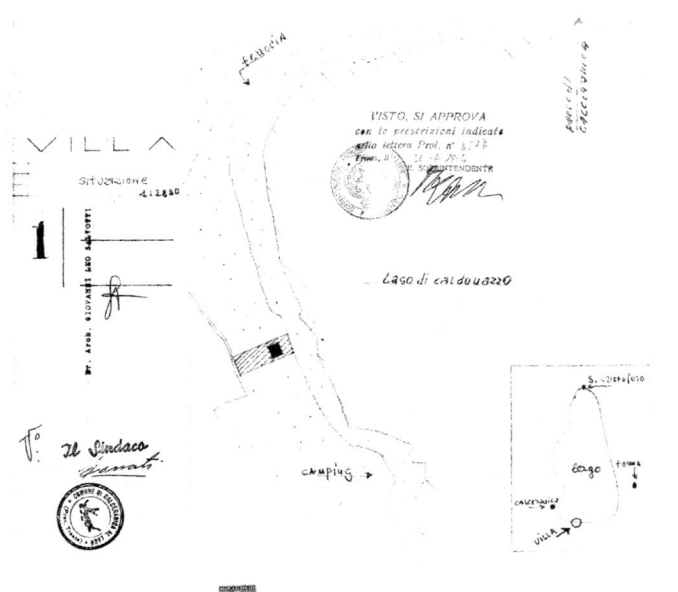

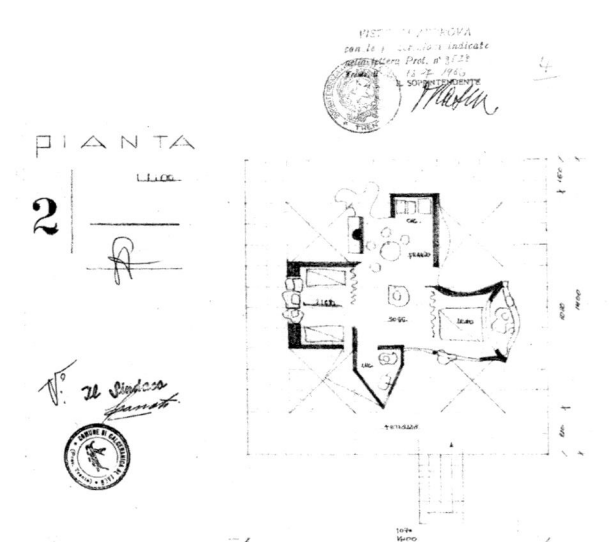

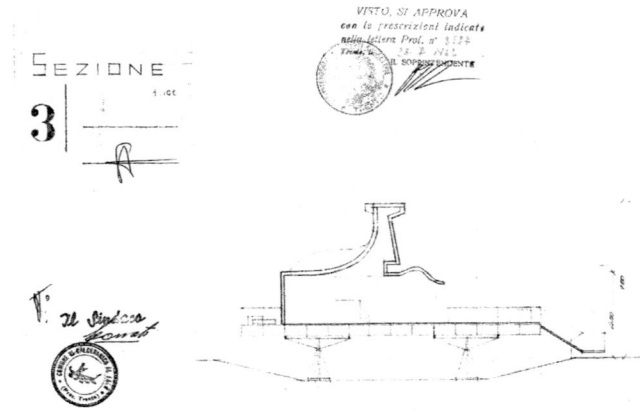

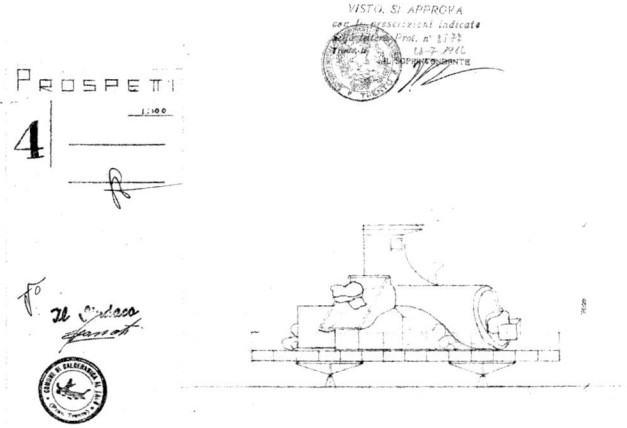

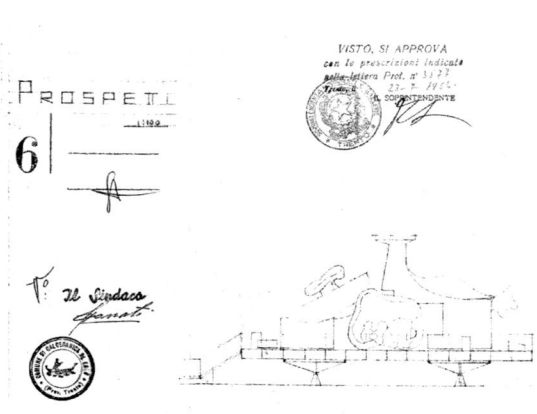

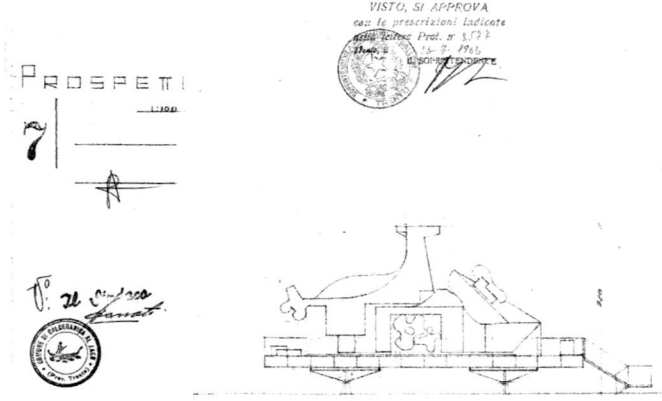

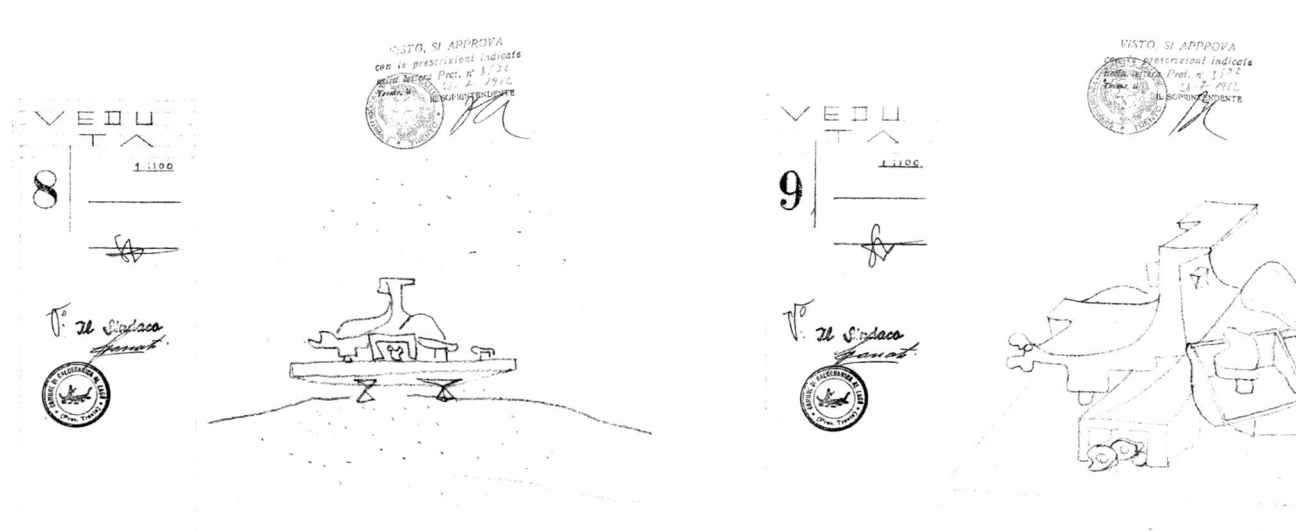

52

Casa Galina. A photo essay

Luca Chistè

56

58

60

64

68

74

76

78

84

86

Bibliographical references

Alberti Leon Battista, *Opere volgari*, vol. II.

Augé Marc, (2004), *Rovine e macerie. Il senso del tempo*, Bollati Boringhieri, Torino.

Camus Albert, (1988), *Opere. Romanzi, racconti, saggi*, Bompiani, Milano.

Cassani Alberto Giorgio, (2000), *La fatica del costruire. Tempo e materia nel pensiero di Leon Battista Alberti*, Edizioni Unicopli, Milano.

Diderot Denis, (1767), *Salon*.

de Chateaubriand François-René (1802), *Génie du Christianisme*, III, 5, 3.

Huyssen Andreas (2010). "Authentic Ruins: Products of Modernity." *In Ruins of Modernity by Julia Hell and Andreas Schönle*, (a cura di), Durham: Duke University Press, pp. 17-28.

Lévi-Strauss Claude, (1982), *Tristi tropici*, Il Saggiatore, Milano.

Pacioni Marco, (2015), "Il pensiero per frammenti", in Barbanera M. e Capodiferro A. (a cura di), *La forza delle rovine*, Electa, Milano.

Purini Franco (2015), "Attualità di Piranesi", in Giovanna A. Massari (a cura di), *Tempo forma immagine dell'architettura. Scritti in onore di Vittorio Ugo*, Officina Edizioni, Roma.

Simmel Georg, (1919), *Gesammelte Essays*, Alfred Kroner Leipzig.

Snodgrass Adrian, (2004), *Architettura, Tempo, Eternità. Il simbolismo degli astri e del tempo nell'architettura della Tradizione*, Bruno Mondadori, Milano.

Segre Cesare, (2003), *La pelle di San Bartolomeo*, Einaudi, Torino.

Credits

The architect

Born in 1931, **Giovanni Leo Salvotti De Bindis** graduates in Architecture at the University of Florence in 1956. Following two years as apprentice at the Adalberto Libera studio in Rome, he returns to Trento to start his own business while teaching in several technical high schools in the city. From 1968 to 1985 he is also President of the Association of Architects of the Trento province and in the 90s he founds the National Institute of Architecture's section in Trento. During his long career, Salvotti designed several buildings among the most significant and iconic of the region's XXth century architecture, both in and out the city of Trento.

The authors

Raffaele Cetto was born in Levico Terme, in the Trentino region, in 1978. After graduating at the Venice University of Architecture (IUAV) in 2007, he entered the Association of Architects in 2008 and started collaborating with GLASS studio from Venice for the project of the city's new Cinema Palace. After that, he worked with the Palerm&Tabares de Nava studio in Santa Cruz de Tenerife on the final project for the Sanbàpolis multifunctional centre in Trento. In 2008 he moves to Ouidah (Benin) to follow the works of the AtoutAfricanArch. it association. Back in Italy, since 2010 he started working with the studioXarchitettura as a freelancer.

Alessandro Franceschini was born in Trento in 1974. He graduated in Architecture and Philosophy and in 2006 he also achieved a PhD in Urbanism at the University of Pisa. For Listlab he published "Sulla città futura" - 9788898774104 (2014), "Dialoghi sull'urbanistica" - 9788898774722 (2015), the monograph "Willy Schweizer, Maria Grazia Piazzetta. Architettura e spazio alpino" - 9788899854027 (2017), "Le questioni del paesaggio" - 9788899854676 (2017) and "Dialoghi sull'Urbanistica 2" - 9788832080292 (2020).

The photographer

Luca Chistè was born in Trento in 1960 and graduated in Sociology of the cultural and communication phenomena with a major in ethno-antropological studies. He has been a photograph since 1980, with a focus on ethno-sociology and landscapes, both natural-anthropic and urban. His photographic work is based on the use of both medium and large size analogical apparatus and digital instruments. Through a tested workflow he manages all the production phases, from the interpretation of the pictures to fine art copyrights.

Time and Architecture
Casa Galina by Giovanni Leo Salvotti

Authors
Alessandro Franceschini
Raffaele Cetto

Pictures
Luca Chistè

Published by
LIStLab
info@listlab.eu
listlab.eu

Editorial Director
Alessandro Martinelli

Translation
Jacopo Marcomeni

Editorial Office
Marta Mariano

Art Director & Production
Blacklist Creative, BCN
blacklist-creative.com

ISBN 9788898774500

Series **BABEL**

Printed and bound in the European Union 2021

All rights reserved
© of LIStLab edition;
© of the author's texts;
© of the author's images.

No part of this book may be reproduced, stored in a retrieval system, or transmitted in any form or by any means, including electronic, mechanical, photocopying, microfilming, recording or otherwise without written permission from the publisher.

Sales, Marketing & Distribution
distribution@listlab.eu
listlab.eu/en/distribuzione/

For more information concerning LIStLab's Scientific Boards please visit the webpage:
listlab.eu/en/boards/

LIStLab is an editorial workshop, based in Europe, that works on contemporary issues. LIStLab not only publishes, but also researches, proposes, promotes, produces, creates networks.

LIStLab is a green company committed to respect the environment. Paper, ink, glues and all processings come from short supply chains and aim at limiting pollution. The print run of books and magazines is based on consumption patterns, thus preventing waste of paper and surpluses. LIStLab aims at increasing the responsibility of authors and the market, towards a new publishing culture based on smarter resource management.